THE OLD TUNE

THE OLD TUNE

Samuel Beckett

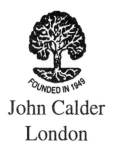

John Calder
London

This edition first published 1999 in Great Britain by
John Calder Publishers
London
La Manivelle first published by Les Editions de Minuit, Paris 1960
English adaptation by Samuel Beckett first published by John
Calder (Publishers) Ltd as *The Old Tune* in *New Writers 2*. 1962,
and subsequently in plays Volume 1 by Robert Pinget by John
Calder (Publishers) Ltd 1963

ISBN 0 7145 43012
Paperback

British Library Cataloguing in Publication Data
A catalogue record for this title is available from the British
Library

Printed in Canada by Webcom Ltd

THE OLD TUNE

Background of street noises. In the foreground a barrel-organ playing an old tune. 20 seconds. The mechanism jams. Thumps on the box to set it off again. No result.

GORMAN (*old man's cracked voice, frequent pauses for breath even in the middle of a word, speech indistinct for want of front teeth, whistling sibilants*). There we go, bust again. (*Sound of lid raised. Scraping inside box.*) Cursed bloody music! (*Scraping. Creaking of handle. Thumps on box. The mechanism starts off again.*) Ah about time!

Tune resumes. 10 seconds. Sound of faltering steps approaching.

CREAM (*old man's cracked voice, stumbling speech, pauses in the middle of sentences, whistling sibilants due to ill-fitting denture*).— Well, if it isn't—(*the tune stops*)—Gorman my old friend Gorman, do you recognize me Cream father of the judge, Cream you remember Cream.

GORMAN. Mr. Cream! Well, I'll be! Mr. Cream! (*Pause.*) Sit you down, sit you down, here, there. (*Pause.*) Great weather for the time of day Mr. Cream, eh.

CREAM. My old friend Gorman, it's a sight to see you again after all these years, all these years.

GORMAN. Yes indeed, Mr. Cream, yes indeed, that's the way it is. (*Pause.*) And you, tell me.

CREAM. I was living with my daughter and she died, then I came here to live with the other.

GORMAN. Miss Miss what?

5

CREAM. Bertha. You know she got married, yes, Moody the nurseryman, two children.

GORMAN. Grand match, Mr. Gorman, grand match, more power to you. But tell me then the poor soul she was taken then was she.

CREAM. Malignant, tried everything, lingered three years, that's how it goes, the young pop off and the old hang on.

GORMAN. Ah dear oh dear Mr. Cream, dear oh dear.

Pause.

CREAM. And you your wife?

GORMAN. Still in it, still in it, but for how long.

CREAM. Poor Daisy yes.

GORMAN. Had she children?

CREAM. Three, three children, Johnny, the eldest, then Ronnie, then a baby girl, Queenie, my favourite, Queenie, a baby girl.

GORMAN. Darling name.

CREAM. She's so quick for her years you wouldn't believe it, do you know what she came out with to me the other day ah only the other day poor Daisy.

GORMAN. And your son-in-law?

CREAM. Eh?

GORMAN. Ah dear oh dear, Mr. Cream, dear oh dear. (*Pause.*) Ah yes children that's the way it is. (*Roar of motor engine.*) They'd tear you to flitters with their flaming machines

CREAM. Shocking crossing, sudden death.

GORMAN. As soon as look at you, tear you to flitters.

CREAM. Ah in our time Gorman this was the outskirts, you remember, peace and quiet.

GORMAN. Do I remember, fields it was, fields, bluebells, over there, on the bank, bluebells. When you think. . . . (*Suddenly complete silence. 10 seconds. The tune resumes, falters, stops. Silence. The street noises resume.*) Ah the horses, the

carriages, and the barouches, ah the barouches, all that's
the dim distant past, Mr. Cream.

CREAM. And the broughams, remember the broughams,
there was style for you, the broughams.

Pause.

GORMAN. The first car I remember well I saw it here, here,
on the corner, a Pic-Pic she was.

CREAM. Not a Pic-Pic, Gorman, not a Pic-Pic, a Dee
Dyan Button.

GORMAN. A Pic-Pic, a Pic-Pic, don't I remember well, just
as I was coming out of Swan's the bookseller's beyond there
on the corner, Swan's the bookseller's that was, just as I was
coming out with a rise of fourpence ah there wasn't much
money in it in those days.

CREAM. A Dee Dyan, a Dee Dyan.

GORMAN. You had to work for your living in those days, it
wasn't at six you knocked off, nor at seven neither, eight it
was, eight o'clock, yes by God. (*Pause.*) Where was I?
(*Pause.*) Ah yes eight o'clock as I was coming out of Swan's
there was the crowd gathered and the car wheeling round the
bend.

CREAM. A Dee Dyan Gorman, a Dee Dyan, I can remember the man himself from Wougham he was the vintner
what's this his name was.

GORMAN. Bush, Seymour Bush.

CREAM. Bush that's the man.

GORMAN. One way or t'other, Mr. Cream, one way or
t'other no matter it wasn't the likes of nowadays, their
flaming machines they'd tear you to shreds.

CREAM. My dear Gorman do you know what it is I'm
going to tell you, all this speed do you know what it is it has
the whole place ruinated, no living with it any more, the
whole place ruinated, even the weather. (*Roar of engine.*) Ah
when you think of the springs in our time remember the

springs we had, the heat there was in them, and the summers remember the summers would destroy you with the heat.

GORMAN. Do I remember, there was one year back there seems like yesterday must have been round 95 when we were still out at Cruddy, didn't we water the roof of the house every evening with the rubber jet to have a bit of cool in the night, yes summer 95.

CREAM. That would surprise me Gorman, remember in those days the rubber hose was a great luxury a great luxury, wasn't till after the war the rubber hose.

GORMAN. You may be right.

CREAM. No may be about it, I tell you the first we ever had round here was in Drummond's place, old Da Drummond, that was after the war 1920 maybe, still very exorbitant it was at the time, don't you remember watering out of the can you must with that bit of a garden you had didn't you, wasn't it your father owned that patch out on the Marston Road.

GORMAN. The Sheen Road Mr. Cream but true for you the watering you're right there, me and me hose how are you when we had no running water at the time or had we.

CREAM. The Sheen Road, that's the one out beyond Shackleton's sawpit.

GORMAN. We didn't get it in till 1925 now it comes back to me the wash-hand basin and jug.

Roar of engine.

CREAM. The Sheen Road you saw what they've done to that I was out on it yesterday with the son-in-law, you saw what they've done our little gardens and the grand sloe hedges.

GORMAN. Yes all those gazebos springing up like thistles there's trash for you if you like, collapse if you look at them am I right.

CREAM. Collapse is the word, when you think of the good

stone made the cathedrals nothing to come up to it.

GORMAN. And on top of all no foundations, no cellars, no nothing, how are you going to live without cellars I ask you, on piles if you don't mind, piles, like in the lake age, there's progress for you.

CREAM. Ah Gorman you haven't changed a hair, just the same old wag he always was. Getting on for seventy-five is it?

GORMAN. Seventy-three, seventy-three, soon due for the knock.

CREAM. Now Gorman none of that, none of that, and me turning seventy-six, you're a young man Gorman.

GORMAN. Ah Mr. Cream, always the great one for a crack.

CREAM. Here Gorman while we're at it have a fag, here. (*Pause.*) The daughter must have whipped them again, doesn't want me to be smoking, mind her own damn business. (*Pause.*) Ah I have them, here, have one.

GORMAN. I wouldn't leave you short.

CREAM. Short for God's sake, here, have one.

Pause.

GORMAN. They're packed so tight they won't come out.

CREAM. Take hold of the packet. (*Pause.*) Ah what ails me all bloody thumbs. Can you pick it up.

Pause.

GORMAN. Here we are. (*Pause.*) Ah yes a nice puff now and again but it's not what it was their gaspers now not worth a fiddler's, remember in the forces the shag remember the black shag that was tobacco for you.

CREAM. Ah the black shag my dear Gorman the black shag, fit for royalty the black shag fit for royalty. (*Pause.*) Have you a light on you.

GORMAN. Well then I haven't, the wife doesn't like me to be smoking.

Pause.

CREAM. Must have whipped my lighter too the bitch, my old tinder jizzer.

GORMAN. Well no matter I'll keep it and have a draw later on.

CREAM. The bitch sure as a gun she must have whipped it too that's going beyond the beyonds, beyond the beyonds, nothing you can call your own. (*Pause.*) Perhaps we might ask this gentleman. (*Footsteps approach.*) Beg your pardon Sir trouble you for a light.

Footsteps recede.

GORMAN. Ah the young nowadays Mr. Cream very wrapped up they are the young nowadays, no thought for the old. When you think, when you think. . . . (*Suddenly complete silence. 10 seconds. The tune resumes, falters, stops. Silence. The street noises resume.*) Where were we? (*Pause.*) Ah yes the forces, you went in in 1900, 1900, 1902, am I right?

CREAM. 1903, 1903, and you 1906 was it?

GORMAN. 1906 yes at Chatham.

CREAM. The Gunners?

GORMAN. The Foot, the Foot.

CREAM. But the Foot wasn't Chatham don't you remember, there it was the Gunners, you must have been at Caterham, Caterham, the Foot.

GORMAN. Chatham I tell you, isn't it like yesterday, Morrison's pub on the corner.

CREAM. Harrison's, Harrison's Oak Lounge, do you think I don't know Chatham. I used to go there on holiday with Mrs. Cream, I know Chatham backwards Gorman, inside and out, Harrison's Oak Lounge on the corner of what was the name of the street, on a rise it was, it'll come back to me, do you think I don't know Harrison's Oak Lounge there on the corner of dammit I'll forget my own name next and the square it'll come back to me.

GORMAN. Morrison or Harrison we were at Chatham.

CREAM. That would surprise me greatly, the Gunners were Chatham do you not remember that?

GORMAN. I was in the Foot, at Chatham, in the Foot.

CREAM. The Foot, that's right the Foot at Chatham.

GORMAN. That's what I'm telling you, Chatham the Foot.

CREAM. That would surprise me greatly, you must have it mucked up with the war, the mobilisation.

GORMAN. The mobilisation have a heart it's as clear in my mind as yesterday the mobilisation, we were shifted straight away to Chesham, was it, no, Chester, that's the place, Chester, there was Morrison's pub on the corner and a chamber-maid, Mr. Cream, a chamber-maid what was her name, Joan, Jean, Jane, the very start of the war when we still didn't believe it, Chester, ah those are happy memories.

CREAM. Happy memories, happy memories, I wouldn't go so far as that.

GORMAN. I mean the start up, the start up at Chatham, we still didn't believe it, and that chamber-maid what was her name it'll come back to me. (*Pause.*) And your son by the same token.

Roar of engine.

CREAM. Eh?

GORMAN. Your son the judge.

CREAM. He has rheumatism.

GORMAN. Ah rheumatism, rheumatism runs in the blood Mr. Cream.

CREAM. What are you talking about, I never had rheumatism.

GORMAN. When I think of my poor old mother, only sixty and couldn't move a muscle. (*Roar of engine.*) Rheumatism they never found the remedy for it yet, atom rockets is all they care about, I can thank my lucky stars touch wood. (*Pause.*) Your son yes he's in the papers the Carton affair, the way he managed that case he can be a proud man, the wife read it again in this morning's *Lark*.

CREAM. What do you mean the Barton affair.

GORMAN The Carton affair Mr. Cream, the sex fiend, on the Assizes.

CREAM. That's not him, he's not the Assizes my boy isn't, he's the County Courts, you mean Judge . . . Judge . . . what's this his name was in the Barton affair.

GORMAN. Ah I thought it was him.

CREAM. Certainly not I tell you, the County Courts my boy, not the Assizes, the County Courts.

GORMAN. Oh you know the Courts and the Assizes it was always all six of one to me.

CREAM. Ah but there's a big difference Mr. Gorman, a power of difference, a civil case and a criminal one, quite another how d'you do, what would a civil case be doing in the *Lark* now I ask you.

GORMAN. All that machinery you know I never got the swing of it and now it's all six of one to me.

CREAM. Were you never in the Courts?

GORMAN. I was once all right when my niece got her divorce that was when was it now thirty years ago yes thirty years, I was greatly put about I can tell you the poor little thing divorced after two years of married life, my sister was never the same after it.

CREAM. Divorce is the curse of society you can take it from me, the curse of society, ask my boy if you don't believe me.

GORMAN. Ah there I'm with you the curse of society look at what it leads up to, when you think my niece had a little girl as good as never knew her father.

CREAM. Did she get alimony.

GORMAN. She was put out to board and wasted away to a shadow, that's a nice thing for you.

CREAM. Did the mother get alimony.

GORMAN. Divil the money. (*Pause.*) So that's your son ladling out the divorces.

CREAM. As a judge he must, as a father it goes to his heart.

GORMAN. Has he children.

CREAM. Well in a way he had one, little Herbert, lived to be four months then passed away, how long is it now, how long is it now.

GORMAN. Ah dear oh dear, Mr. Cream, dear oh dear and did they never have another?

Roar of engine.

CREAM. Eh?

GORMAN. Other children.

CREAM. Didn't I tell you, I have my daughters' children, my two daughters. (*Pause.*) Talking of that your man there Barton the sex boyo isn't that nice carryings on for you showing himself off like that without a stitch on him to little children might just as well have been ours Gorman, our own little grandchildren.

Roar of engine.

GORMAN. Mrs. Cream must be a proud woman too to be a grandmother.

CREAM. Mrs. Cream is in her coffin these twenty years Mr. Gorman.

GORMAN. Oh God forgive me what am I talking about, I'm getting you wouldn't know what I'd be talking about, that's right you were saying you were with Miss Daisy.

CREAM. With my daughter Bertha, Mr. Gorman, my daughter Bertha, Mrs. Rupert Moody.

GORMAN. Your daughter Bertha that's right so she married Moody, gallous garage they have there near the slaughter-house.

CREAM. Not him, his brother the nursery-man.

H

GORMAN. Grand match, more power to you, have they children?

Roar of engine.

CREAM. Eh?

GORMAN. Children.

CREAM. Two dotey little boys, little Johnny I mean Hubert and the other, the other.

GORMAN. But tell me your daughter poor soul she was taken then was she. (*Pause.*) That cigarette while we're at it might try this gentleman. (*Footsteps approach.*) Beg your pardon Sir trouble you for a light. (*Footsteps recede.*) Ah the young are very wrapped up Mr. Cream.

CREAM. Little Hubert and the other, the other, what's this his name is. (*Pause.*) And Mrs. Gorman.

GORMAN. Still in it.

CREAM. Ah you're the lucky jim Gorman, you're the lucky jim, Mrs. Gorman by gad, fine figure of a woman Mrs. Gorman, fine handsome woman.

GORMAN. Handsome, all right, but you know, age. We have our health thanks be to God touch wood. (*Pause.*) You know what it is Mr. Cream, that'd be the way to pop off chatting away like this of a sunny morning.

CREAM. None of that now Gorman, who's talking of popping off with the health you have as strong as an ox and a comfortable wife, ah I'd give ten years of mine to have her back do you hear me, living with strangers isn't the same.

GORMAN. Miss Bertha's so sweet and good you're on the pig's back for God's sake, on the pig's back.

CREAM. It's not the same you can take it from me, can't call your soul your own, look at the cigarettes, the lighter.

GORMAN. Miss Bertha so sweet and good.

CREAM. Sweet and good, all right, but dammit if she doesn't take me for a doddering old drivelling dotard. (*Pause.*) What did I do with those cigarettes?

GORMAN. And tell me your poor dear daughter-in-law what am I saying your daughter-in-law.

CREAM. My daughter-in-law, my daughter-in-law, what about my daughter-in-law.

GORMAN. She had private means, it was said she had private means.

CREAM. Private means ah they were the queer private means, all swallied up in the war every ha'penny do you hear me, all in the bank the private means not as much land as you'd tether a goat. (*Pause.*) Land Gorman there's no security like land but that woman you might as well have been talking to the bedpost, a mule she was that woman was.

GORMAN. Ah well it's only human nature, you can't always pierce into the future.

CREAM. Now now Gorman don't be telling me, land wouldn't you live all your life off a bit of land damn it now wouldn't you any fool knows that unless they take the fantasy to go and build on the moon the way they say, ah that's all fantasy Gorman you can take it from me all fantasy and delusion, they'll smart for it one of these days by God they will.

GORMAN. You don't believe in the moon what they're experimenting at.

CREAM. My dear Gorman the moon is the moon and cheese is cheese what do they take us for, didn't it always exist the moon wasn't it always there as large as life and what did it ever mean only fantasy and delusion Gorman, fantasy and delusion. (*Pause.*) Or is it our forefathers were a lot of old bags maybe now is that on the cards I ask you, Bacon, Wellington, Washington, for them the moon was always in their opinion damn it I ask you you'd think to hear them talk no one ever bothered his arse with the moon before, make a cat swallow his whiskers they think they've discovered the moon as if as if. (*Pause.*) What was I driving at?

Roar of engine.

GORMAN. So you're against progress are you.

CREAM. Progress, progress, progress is all very fine and grand, there's such a thing I grant you, but it's scientific, progress, scientific, the moon's not progress, lunacy, lunacy.

GORMAN. Ah there I'm with you progress is scientific and the moon, the moon, that's the way it is.

CREAM. The wisdom of the ancients that's the trouble they don't give a rap or a snap for it any more, and the world going to rack and ruin, wouldn't it be better now to go back to the old maxims and not be gallivanting off killing one another in China over the moon, ah when I think of my poor father.

GORMAN. Your father that reminds me I knew your father well. (*Roar of engine.*) There was a man for you old Mr. Cream, what he had to say he lashed out with it straight from the shoulder and no humming and hawing, now it comes back to me one one year there on the town council my father told me must have been wait now till I see 95, 95 or 6, a short while before he resigned, 95 that's it the year of the great frost.

CREAM. Ah I beg your pardon, the great frost was 93 I'd just turned ten, 93 Gorman the great frost.

Roar of engine.

GORMAN. My father used to tell the story how Mr. Cream went hell for leather for the mayor who was he in those days, must have been Overend yes Overend.

CREAM. Ah there you're mistaken my dear Gorman, my father went on the council with Overend in 97, January 97.

GORMAN. That may be, that may be, but it must have been 95 or 6 just the same seeing as how my father went off in 96, April 96, there was a set against him and he had to give in his resignation.

CREAM. Well then your father was off when it happened, all I know is mine went on with Overend in 97 the year Marable was burnt out.

GORMAN. Ah Marrable it wasn't five hundred yards from the door five hundred yards Mr. Cream, I can still hear my poor mother saying to us ah poor dear Maria she was saying to me again only last night, January 96 that's right.

CREAM. 97 I tell you, 97, the year my father was voted on.

GORMAN. That may be but just the same the clout he gave Overend that's right now I have it.

CREAM. The clout was Oscar Bliss the butcher in Pollox Street.

GORMAN. The butcher in Pollox Street, there's a memory from the dim distant past for you, didn't he have a daughter do you remember.

CREAM. Helen, Helen Bliss, pretty girl, she'd be my age, 83 saw the light of day.

GORMAN. And Rosie Plumpton bonny Rosie staring up at the lid these thirty years she must be now and Molly Berry and Eva what was her name Eva Hart that's right Eva Hart didn't she marry a Crumplin.

CREAM. Her brother, her brother Alfred married Gertie Crumplin great one for the lads she was you remember, Gertie great one for the lads.

GORMAN. Do I remember, Gertie Crumplin great bit of skirt by God, hee hee hee great bit of skirt.

CREAM. You old dog you!

Roar of engine.

GORMAN. And Nelly Crowther there's one came to a nasty end.

CREAM. Simon's daughter that's right, the parents were greatly to blame you can take it from me.

GORMAN. They reared her well then just the same bled themselves white for her so they did, poor Mary used to tell us all we were very close in those days lived on the same landing you know, poor Mary yes she used to say what a drain it was having the child boarding out at Saint Theresa's can you imagine, very classy, daughters of the gentry Mr. Cream, even taught French they were the young ladies.

CREAM. Isn't that what I'm telling you, reared her like a princess of the blood they did, French now I ask you, French.

GORMAN. Would you blame them Mr. Cream, the best of parents, you can't deny it, education.

CREAM. French, French, isn't that what I'm saying.

Roar of engine.

GORMAN. They denied themselves everything, take the bits out of their mouths they would for their Nelly.

CREAM. Don't be telling me they had her on a string all the same the said young lady, remember that Holy Week 1912 was it or 13.

Roar of engine.

GORMAN. Eh?

CREAM. When you think of Simon the man he was don't be telling me that. (*Pause.*) Holy Week 1913 now it all comes back to me is that like as if they had her on a string what she did then.

GORMAN. Peace to her ashes Mr. Cream.

CREAM. Principles, Gorman, principles without principles I ask you. (*Roar of engine.*) Wasn't there an army man in it.

GORMAN. Eh?

CREAM. Wasn't there an army man in it.

GORMAN. In the car?

CREAM. Eh?

GORMAN. An army man in the car?

CREAM. In the Crowther blow-up.

Roar of engine.

GORMAN. You mean the Lootnant St. John Fitzball.

CREAM. St. John Fitzball that's the man, wasn't he mixed up in it?

GORMAN. They were keeping company all right. (*Pause.*) He died in 14. Wounds.

CREAM. And his aunt Miss Hester.

GORMAN. Dead then these how many years is it now how many.

CREAM. She was a great old one, a little on the high and mighty side perhaps you might say.

GORMAN. Take fire like gunpowder but a heart of gold if you only knew. (*Roar of engine.*) Her niece has a chip of the old block wouldn't you say.

CREAM. Her niece? No recollection.

GORMAN. No recollection, Miss Victoria, come on now, she was to have married an American and she's in the Turrets yet.

CREAM. I thought they'd sold.

GORMAN. Sell the Turrets is it they'll never sell, the family seat three centuries and maybe more, three centuries Mr. Cream.

CREAM. You might be their historiographer Gorman to hear you talk, what you don't know about those people.

GORMAN. Histryographer no Mr. Cream I wouldn't go so far as that but Miss Victoria right enough I know her through and through we stop and have a gas like when her aunt was still in it, ah yes nothing hoity-toity about Miss Victoria you can take my word she has a great chip of the old block.

CREAM. Hadn't she a brother.

GORMAN. The Lootnant yes died, in 14. Wounds.

Deafening roar of engine.

CREAM. The bloody cars such a thing as a quiet chat I ask

you. (*Pause.*) Well I'll be slipping along I'm holding you back from your work.

GORMAN. Slipping along what would you want slipping along and we only after meeting for once in a blue moon.

CREAM. Well then just a minute and smoke a quick one. (*Pause.*) What did I do with those cigarettes? (*Pause.*) You fire ahead don't mind me.

GORMAN. When you think, when you think. . . .

Suddenly complete silence. 10 seconds. Resume and submerge tune a moment. Street noises and tune together crescendo. Tune finally rises above them triumphant.

POSTFACE

The circumstances of the writing of *The Old Tune* are of some interest because it is the only time that Samuel Beckett translated a play by a contemporary. Beckett and Robert Pinget knew each other well and when Pierre Chabert, the actor and director, was asked to stage Pinget's play *Hypothèse* for the Petit Odéon by Jean-Louis Barrault, there were so many difficulties that he turned to Beckett for help. Beckett was able to come up with a series of stage ideas and directions that made the play a considerable success within the world of French avant-garde theatre. The relationship between the two writers, who shared a publisher and much else in terms of style and outlook, had on that account a professional aspect as well as friendship.

Beckett was, however, never keen to allow his own work to be adapted for other media. He allowed *Godot* to be adapted for television by Donald McWhinnie, purely out of friendship, but was not happy with the result. He refused all film offers for his plays and for adaptations of the novels. When Laurence Olivier had the idea of staging the radio play *All That Fall* at the National Theatre he assumed that permission would be automatic and the play was already in rehearsal before permission was formally requested from the theatrical agent who handled Beckett's plays in Britain. Olivier was astounded when permission was refused, and went to Paris with Joan Littlewood, his wife, who was cast to play the principle role, in order to persuade Beckett to allow them to proceed. At an otherwise pleasant dinner, the author explained how the play was based on sounds: the significance of footsteps, the noises of farmyard animals, train whistles and other aural effects which would be lost in a visual production. The Oliviers reluctantly had to agree to cancel the production.

When RTF wished to present *All That Fall* in French, Beckett was himself unable to undertake the translation and Robert

Pinget was asked to do it, and although reluctant to do so Beckett gave permission. But to indicate as subtly as possible his dislike of having his work adapted by others, he took Pinget's own radio play *La Manivelle* and changed it to a very different background but with similar characters who were familiar to him from his youth. A very French play became a British one, but it is not clear, from the language spoken by the two protagonists exactly where it is set. The language used has an Irish resonance, but not entirely, and the camps where the two old soldiers were stationed are all in England. It can therefore be assumed that the Beckett version could be set anywhere in the British Isles, but as the events remembered would be long before Irish independence, it may well be in Ireland.

In its simple way it is a masterpiece, faithful in tone to the original conception, but still very much a part of the Beckett theatrical canon. Robert Pinget took the hint and thereafter never undertook to adapt any other Beckett text.